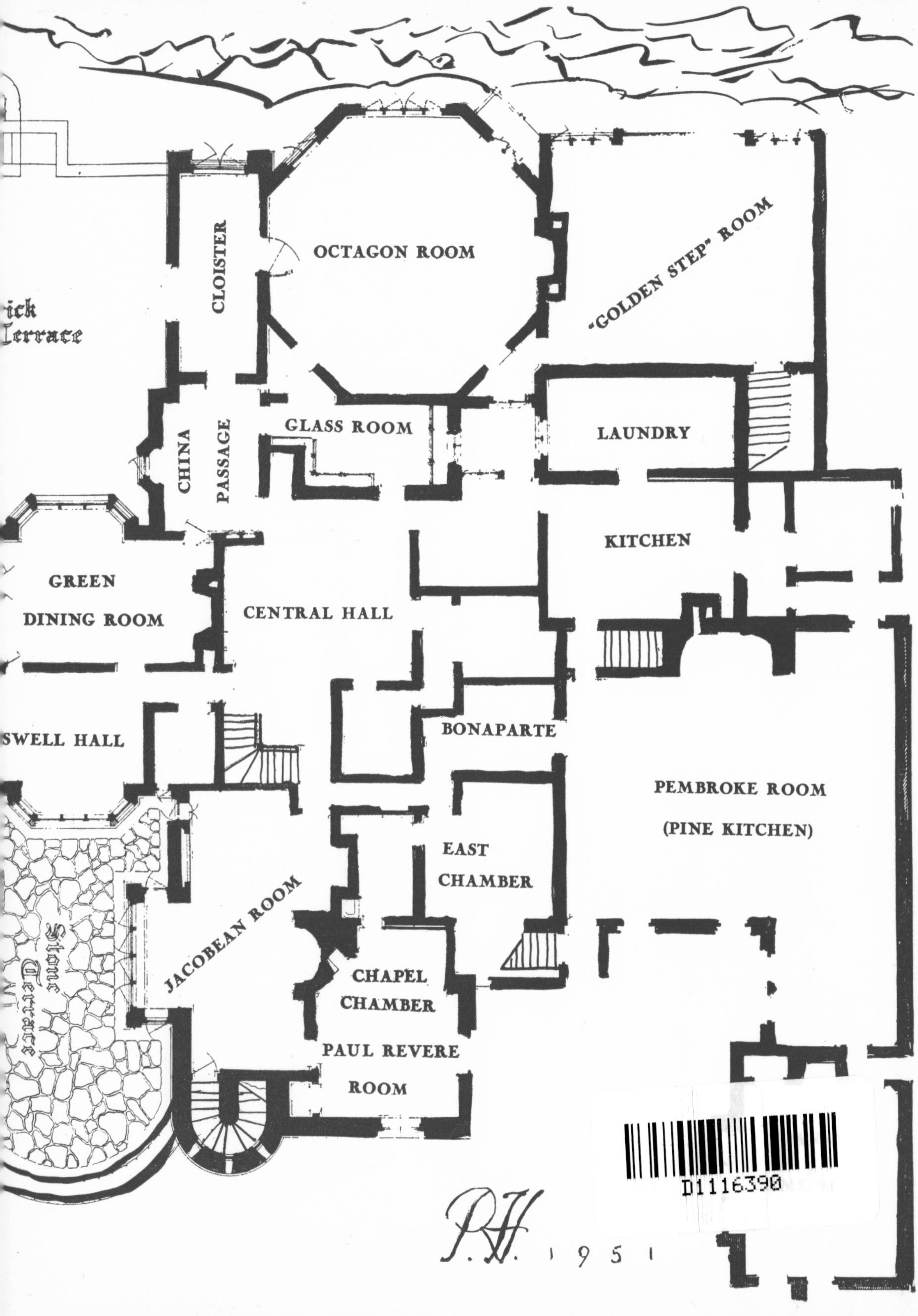

OCTAGON ROOM

CLOISTER

"GOLDEN STEP" ROOM

ick
Terrace

CHINA PASSAGE

GLASS ROOM

LAUNDRY

KITCHEN

GREEN

DINING ROOM

CENTRAL HALL

SWELL HALL

BONAPARTE

PEMBROKE ROOM

(PINE KITCHEN)

EAST

CHAMBER

Stone
Terrace

JACOBEAN ROOM

CHAPEL

CHAMBER

PAUL REVERE

ROOM

P.H. 1951

BEAUPORT

THE STRAWBERRY HILL ROOM

BEAUPORT

at GLOUCESTER

The most FASCINATING *house in America*

The PICTURES *by* SAMUEL CHAMBERLAIN
The WORDS *by* PAUL HOLLISTER

HASTINGS HOUSE · *Publishers* · NEW YORK

FOREWORD

By agreement in June 1942, Constance, Frasier and Helena, children of Mrs. Helena W. McCann transferred "Beauport" to the Society for the Preservation of New England Antiquities, with an annual grant for maintenance from the Winfield Foundation, to make the house permanently available for the benefit and education of the public as a memorial to their mother.

So in December the deed and details of this extremely generous, well-considered and interesting gift were duly recorded. The Society took on the responsibility for its 44th property, in a roster that now numbers 56. They stand, hospitably, in five of the six New England states, ranging from the sturdy dwellings of the seventeenth and eighteenth centuries, through the impressive mansions of the Federal period, to the fine homes of the early Republic. Most are open to the public. All of them are preserved and furnished through the interest and generosity of members and friends of the Society.

In 1950, the Society chanced to bring together at its headquarters (the Harrison Gray Otis House, 141 Cambridge Street, in Boston) one of the country's finest picture-makers and a writer who had known Henry Davis Sleeper, the creator of "Beauport" and had learned from him first-hand the story of the house. The happy result follows.

They have told you in pictures and words how a twentieth-century genuis has strikingly re-created in a series of rooms full of antiquities and glowing with colour, many of the moods and mingled skeins of culture that have contributed to the tapestry of our America.

BERTRAM K. LITTLE, *Director*
The Society for the Preservation
of New England Antiquities

Beauport

With this book, a small piece of land, a little money, a weakness for collecting odd things, a gift of putting them together in the right places, a reasonable sense of colour and comfort, a liking for pleasant people, and the simple rudiments of architectural sense — you, too, can possess some part of the most fascinating house in America, as Henry Sleeper achieved the whole of it. And the money isn't the talisman, nor the bar.

It won't handicap you to have been to France, though this is in no way necessary. Sleeper had. Only the exterior of his house was much influenced by France. When he went to Paris he did so as a student, in the late Nineties. His grandfather had left him enough money to let him choose his own career. He studied architecture and came home to Boston.

Why he went into a publishing house instead of practicing architecture I never asked. Maybe he didn't like the bricks-and-mortar and the trigonometry and drudgery of conventional building. Certainly he was much more interested in the living that goes on within a house than with the neighbor's-eye view of the outside of it. Someone suggested that he may have been a frustrated painter, whose craving for colour and composition finally reacted into masterpieces as rooms inside houses. I'm pretty sure that he was aware that in 1604, Samuel Champlain had discovered the Massachusetts haven we now call Gloucester on Cape Ann, had mapped and named it *Beau Port,* or "Handsome Harbour."

As a bachelor in Boston, Sleeper thought he ought to have a little place of his own on the North Shore, at a spot where privacy would prevail, the elements comply, and guests compose. He built a clean modest little harbour-side shingle cottage near the tip of Eastern Point at Gloucester — Champlain's sheltered deep-water refuge. The cottage resembled perhaps a million others along the Atlantic seaboard. But in honour of Samuel Champlain, and with a homesick nod to his own student life on the Left Bank, Sleeper named his cottage "Beauport" — a sort of fancy title, but a lot better than Kamp Kill Kare.

Driving one day through the bleached shipbuilding village of Essex, he saw a notice that the tottering William Cogswell house was up for sale — one of those early 18th-century houses huddled down like a grizzled cat on the edge of the salt hay. To the real-estater Sleeper said: "You have a fat offer for the panelling and flooring. You will make more money if you accept the offer. But if you do, it will go to New York. I can offer you little, but with my offer goes my promise that if you sell this woodwork to me, it will move no more than a few miles from Essex, and I shall install it in a house where it will keep its dignity, among its own people. That may be worth thinking twice about."

The man thought twice, and the panelling of the front hall of the William Cogswell house was hauled over to Beauport, the little shingled cottage on Eastern Point. Sleeper got out his pencil and paper and T-square, and presently the cottage had a new front hall, panelled in pine nearly two centuries old. To be sure, the cottage then had not much else. But that new hall, you might say, was the cornerstone of Henry Davis Sleeper, the Genius.

For Beauport today contains upwards of 40 rooms, provocatively unusual. In the years before World War I the cottage slowly expanded along a pattern of imagination which became a sort of working policy. Stated as simply as Mr. Sleeper once put it to me, the scheme was this:

"Mightn't it be fun to have a house in which each room could recapture some of the spirit of a specific mood or phase or 'period' of our American life from the time of Plymouth down through the Revolution and the early Republic?"

To cause such a house, livable and without dogmatism, became his career. People with wits began to visit him, and began to talk volubly about him.

Singly, or in compatible clusters, came the ladies and gentlemen of the arts: the sculptors Ladd and Manship and McKenzie; the architects Cram and Lindeberg; the painters and illustrators Beaux and John and Hopkinson and Cady and Chamberlain and Arnoux; the writers Glasgow and Hedin and Churchill and Wister and Benet and Tarkington, Marquand and Howe and Siegfried and Drinker-Bowen and Street; the playwrights O'Neill and Howard and Heyward. There came one day the sunny-twilit "Grave Alice" Longfellow. There came the ladies and gentlemen of music: Gluck and Zimbalist and Hess and Samaroff and Stokowski and Barlow; the ladies of wit-and-muscle Curtis and Sears; the theatre people like Hayes and Coward, Heming, Eames and Robson and Janis, Barrymore, Yurka, and Eldredge and March, Draper and Marbury, Monterey and Boland, and Tree and Manners; the electronic scientists John Hays Hammond, Jr., and Alexanderson; the statesmen Marshall (a Vice President), and Jusserand and Riano and Morgan and Bliss and Bullitt (ambassadors), and Fuller (a governor), and Lodge, a senator from Beverly. There came the generals Edwards and MacNider and Passaga (who said he was *"emerveillé"*). The men of capital, too — Stotesbury and Astor and Field and Leiter and duPont and Macaulay; Bishop Rhinelander; the bright ladies, Bessie Merryman and Helen Frick and Esther Welles (who signed her home address in the guest-book as "Boston Storage Warehouse"). Eleanor Roosevelt was there, for she got around, way back even then, and Pauline Thayer, who was descended directly and gracefully from Paul Revere. And naturally there came all the real "greats" of current decoration: Elsie deWolfe, Nancy McClelland, Ruby Ross Wood, Hobe Erwin, Dorothy Draper, and Francis Gilbert, a dozen more — they came again and again. Dull moments were few and far between.

In 1914 France went to war, and the summer house called "Beauport" became an exercise for the left hand only. A bold patriot named Piatt Andrew, who was Sleeper's neighbor on the harbour, was as aroused as he by the crisis of France. So was a New York banker named Bill Hereford. These three musketeers thereupon organized, staffed, and supplied the American Field Service, to run ambulances to *postes de sécour* and field hospitals behind the French front lines. You remember how, like the Lafayette Escadrille, the Field Service became a *corps élite* ahead of the van of Pershing's American Expeditionary Forces.

The devotion Sleeper paid to the A.F.S. took all his time for five years and practically cleaned him out of capital. In 1919, with the war past, the Field Service decided to cement Franco-American relations tighter by endowing scholarships for French and American boys in opposite colleges. Sleeper set the ball rolling by paying for four himself — one of which he named for my brother, George. Then he took a good look at his checkbook, and found the news bleak. Fresh Sleeper capital was indicated, and soon, or else.

Sleeper liked good food and good talk. He had financed plenty of both in the peace years. The guests who beat a path to his door had gone away hypnotized and covetous. They were astonished by the ingenuity of his interior architecture and decorative imagination. They were charmed by the modest scale of it, for none of it was monumental; you could fit a good-sized Quonset hut over the whole place. Some of the visitors were people who had plenty of money. Would he not, please, *please,* "do something" for them? they would ask.

The war had kept him far too busy for that. Now, however, with a queasy eye on his bank, he undertook a job. A newcomer to a gilded resort (we may call it Oceana) wanted a house with which to crash the Inner Circle. The newcomer put his beach-head problem up to Sleeper. Sleeper said he'd try.

D-Day, the day of house-warming, was bedlam. Curtain-fixers hung fabrics and bagged them in breakaway muslin shrouds while floor-finishers polished floors. A platoon of gardeners stuck a carpet of wired fresh blossoms into an artificial terrace-lawn so that the lights from the marquee would bathe a nocturnal garden. The skeptics of Oceana came, gaped, and were enchanted to discover moods of Early Americana which had never been seen on this gilded reach of shore. The new host was indisputably "in."

This was the first of a stream of commissions. Each Sleeper discharged with virtuosity: houses, apartments, rooms, shops. What they really meant to the man was revenue to spend on Beauport. The house on Gloucester's harbour began to burgeon into the magical maze you visit today.

To itemize and to describe each room in poor words is next to impossible; to set down an insurance appraisal would be little short of capital crime.

The floor plan itself is a labyrinth. Our end-papers show the ground floor only. It outlines a sort of jungle of rooms, a sort of cockeyed double-H, or architectural domino-game. The rooms are generally small, some almost minute. The building may be called two stories high, but with qualifications. It sits high on an orange-grey granite ledge in a snug, shaded garden, except that on the west, it pulls the water of the harbour up over its ankles. The exterior, as has been said, is of French stimulation, but by no means what most people mean by "French." For it is a rumple-roofed, half-timbered, tile-topped confection of dark pink brick and native stone, hewn-and-carved brackets and beams, with impish caps and spiral-brick chimneys, and with glazed Norman cats and squirrels, with towers and dormers, and scarves of ivy and woodbine; it is skirted by terraces and low walls, with punctuations of belfries and hooded shrines. If you've ever sat in the courtyard of the Inn of William the Conqueror at Dîves-sur-Mer in Normandy, you will understand

3

perfectly the scheme of confusion of galleries, the off-beat rhythm of the interruptions of the line and mass of the house; if you've ever read F. Hopkinson Smith's *An Affair at An Inn* (which he wrote at and concerning the Inn at Dîves) you may find the style somewhat forecast. It sounds perfectly awful. It is in fact wholly exciting in the unity and perfection of its syncopated dishevelment and textures.

Let's go in now. . . .

Let's go in from the lane which saunters out toward the Eastern Point light. The wall is impenetrable, except where a life-size sheet-iron Red Indian stands at the gate, holding a sign reading Beauport, and pointing a solid lead forefinger to the gate-cabin, which has a pepper-pot on top, and is open at both ends, its interior whitewashed. Its wall is decorated with a brave coloured ship-eagle all gold and red and blue. Out the houseward end of this shelter, a curving garden-path leads you perhaps twenty steps to the front door, which is itself under a small gable-canopy. At your left on a low mossy wall is a miniature castle in cement, and frequently beside it is a live toad known in the family as Mr. Toad of Toad Hall. You pull a wrought-iron bell. It jangles. Mr. Toad hops two inches. You are greeted by a smiling blue-eyed lady whose name is Mary Wonson. Mary came here first to "do" in 1909, when the house was "Little Beauport" and had only 26 rooms. In my book, Mrs. George Wonson is the Queen of Gloucester, the Empress of Essex County. (George is the Emperor.)

You're now in the Cogswell Room — the hall that came from Essex. It is perhaps 8 by 12 feet, low-ceiled, its only light a leaded bow-window with a large round drop-leaf table before it. Opposite, a tall mahogany cabinet of florid line, displays a rare panoply of Chinese "Export Porcelain" made for the Portuguese gentry 150 years ago or more — a relevant link with the strong Portuguese heritage of Gloucester-town today. The Essex panelling is painted a dull ivory; the floor is of dark waxed-brick. The objects begin to drive you faintly insane. That was part of the Sleeper strategy: to establish the "mood" of a room, and give you a little time to conjure it, and to orient yourself. You remark a tall jar with a dozen walking sticks of whale and swordfish and Nailsea glass and scrimshaw. Behind a cupboard panel are a dozen ladies' parasols, ruffled silk parasols, handy if you want to take the air. . . . The mood has now come upon you. You give up. You'll go anywhere now — submissively.

You are gently prodded into a room hardly larger than the hall, bright with the harbour-light from a bow-window. Its panelled walls (likewise of Cogswell origin) are cool and soothing, in the tone of green you read on the back of a laurel leaf. Another circular drop-leaf table sits in the bow. On it are three "Export Porcelain" serving dishes — like the group we just saw in the hall (they are excerpts from the celebrated McCann collections now shared by the Boston Museum of Fine Arts and the Metropolitan in New York). A tall goblet of mercury glass holds a single fresh pineapple, the Colonial symbol of domestic welcome. A ledge opposite is laden with bright copper, above a gate-leg table on which you gasp somewhat at a double-octagon framed pattern of a myriad tiny sea-shells. This was Beauport's first dining-room. When you swing wide the arched door of a scalloped cupboard, you reveal a collection of rare china, looking for all the world like fresh vivid wedding-flowers, waiting in a cool place.

4

"Let's go out on the terrace," someone says. "It's pleasant there today." It is also pleasant in some 30 other rooms.

It would likewise be pleasant, if time afforded, to linger in the Central Hall just off the Cogswell entrance. The Central Hall has six exits and entrances, plus an angled staircase. This sounds trafficky, though the room is not. In an alcove of its north wall, a leaded Connecticut doorway has become a sort of shallow show-window, like an old shop-front. It is backed with ground glass. On its glass shelves is a studied bombardment of 130 pieces of early brown and amber and yellow-golden glass, in all manner of shapes and tones: flasks and lamps and vases and pipes and beakers, glinting against the light. As a pattern and collection it is unique. There is a legend that a lady from San Francsico, who fancies such glass, once swooned here, and was restored with aromatic salts. When she was revived she noticed, let into a nearby wall, also with an illuminated glass backing, a smaller Connecticut front-doorway, complete with fanlight and leaded side-lights. As her focus returned, she observed that the conventional bull's-eyes of the side-lights of both doorways were not bottle-bottom bull's-eyes at all. Instead, they were pressed Sandwich clear-glass cup-plates, some bearing a historical medallion. Behind each, the back-lighting filtering through the texture of the cup-plate, stood a bit of glassware in various soft colours, so the illusion became that of Sandwich cup-plates in pink and vaseline yellow and violet and amber and amethyst, which would be so rare as to be unheard-of. The lady is reported to have fainted once more, uttering the thin, distant whimper of a gull over Norman's Woe.

It was lucky for her at the time that she did not perceive the working cast-iron stove opposite. It is a miniature statue of George Washington standing on a classic base. Washington is wrapped in a chaste iron sheet, as a Roman senator. "You must come some time in the autumn," said Mr. Sleeper. "George's whole body is the heat-chamber of the contraption. It's wonderful to sit here and see him get hot. He is slow to anger, but so comforting."

Wait: hadn't we set out for the terrace?

Well, the terrace *is* pleasant, and no mistake. The harbour spreads 180 degrees before you, across to the mainland with John Hays Hammond's Gothic abbey marking the shoreline. Southwestward, a long rifle-shot away, is the rock on which Longfellow wrecked the Hesperus, its skipper and his daughter. North lie the Gloucester docks, with the town steeples on the skyline, and with Five Pound Island and Ten Pound Island in the far foreground, and even here you can smell Gloucester's gold — the salt fish — if the wind's right. You lie in the sun, and study the rumpus of galleries and gables and chimneys on the roof line, and hear the lapping of the water on the rocks, and smell the iodine in the rockweed, and you declare you do not believe one solitary word of it.

But you'll find that the magic of the place is real. People *live* here. They even eat. There are in fact five rooms in which one may dine. The green one we just came through, the room with the uranium-mine filled with china, was not set for a meal, so evidently we are not to eat there. We shall, however, pass through a second dining-room on our way to the third. The others we may see later, if we live.

The Octagon Room, just north of our terrace, doesn't look like a dining-room. For luncheon it isn't, except in the autumn or winter, or at the caprice of the host. All five connect directly with the kitchen, so the caprice can be readily gratified.

The room you lucky people are now entering is eight-sided, and like any self-respecting octagon, all the walls are equal. Sleeper had been inspired by the octagon at the Indian Hill, Ben: Perley Poor's rambling mansion at West Newbury. (Ben: Perley always spelt his name Ben: Perley, with the colon where it is.) Probably that is why Sleeper wanted an octagon room, too. From wall to wall it is 20 feet. It is not, you see, a large room. But it is a room which seems to crackle with red and black and gold and pink. The panelled walls and all the woodwork are painted a deep plum colour, so dark as to appear almost black. The ceiling, which is gored, and pitched ever so slightly upwards to the center, is white. Everything else in the room seems to be red and gold-amber.

The woodwork of each alternate wall is capped by what the architects call a broken pediment — the sort of eagle-wing Cupid's-bow heading which you see over the doors of banks, post offices, and Georgian drawing-rooms. In the center of each pediment is a small pedestal, on which in Georgian days sat little Greek and Roman busts, sneering sideways. No busts here. On two of the little overdoor pedestals, facing each other across the room, sit scarlet French tôle-ware tin urns; on the alternate two sit vermilion glass globes. The red-on-black in the woodwork is the key that pitches this improbable room.

All the furniture is made of "tiger" or violin maple. On the floor is an octagonal hooked rug of a pinkish persuasion and on this island stands an octagonal table of fiddle-maple, which Sleeper designed and Mr. Poole, the Gloucesterman, executed. In the center of the table stands an urn of scarlet tôle with a sprig of fresh cedar twigs in it; on the table lie a dozen folio volumes bound in scarlet morocco with bird-tracks of gold tooling. This is the focal center of the room; this is the dining-table when there are only eight, and when it's cold and dark outside, the warm colours sparkle in candle-light from the dark walls. At the right, a high-waisted sideboard of maple bears candles, tray, decanters, teapot, all of tôle. Beyond the sideboard a tall three-panel Chinese screen of lacquer-red half conceals the doorway yonder.

The firebreast is likewise plum-black, with bright brass columns at the grate. An oval French pastel of a good-looking redcoat commands it. Next to the fireplace at our left stands a smallish table and upon it a Chinese red-lacquer peep-show. Like the big table, most of the chairs are of striped maple, seated either in rushes or in mulberry-and-pink-and-black-and-white chintz.

All this you've taken in as you paused at the threshold. You wonder why the dancing light on the ceiling is not white but pink. It is because the awnings, lowered already against the western light, bouncing indoors off the surface of the harbour, are under-lined with *turkey red* calico. Sleeper put the sun to work for him whenever he could. He even put old-fashioned herringbone shutters into the window casings, where they stand folded back, but where you can see that each strap of the diagonal lattice is painted red on black.

You make the short traverse of 20 feet across the room to pass around the edge of the red-lacquer screen at the open door. You see that the doorways and windows are lined with narrow strip-draperies of Portuguese wool-serge, with chintz-like white-and-pink roses on a wine-coloured ground. The intimation of magenta and violet in the draperies is a deliberate signal, a subtle conditioning in your transition to the next room.

The moment you turn past the screen, the transition is accented. You enter a passage barely six feet by three. Its only function is to conduct you. But it has a dark wall, and into that wall, Sleeper let a pointed-top mullioned window, backed by ground glass. You are brought up standing because the window shelves display a breath-taking grouping of pedigreed objects of juicy amethyst glass, made in the days when folks used manganese to make white glass, and now weathered all the way from palest violet to deep Tyrian purple. A stack of fat, red morocco volumes lying on a maple table below this window echoes the room you've just left — but the purple glass has now cooled you off, prepared you for your next surprise.

Through a swing door, you're suddenly transported to an enclosed Riviera terrace. Three walls and ceiling are white plaster, on the fourth wall the tall windows have slid down out of sight into pockets. A square-rigged model of the ship "Golden Step" six feet long, lines the shoreward side of the room. You face, on the north side, twin carvings from a Clipper's stern, and each side and between them shelves loaded with dark-green Wedgwood and Majolica Ware disguised as leaves of cabbage and lettuce. At your left, a long thin, white refectory table stands snug under the open windows. More green leaf-plates dress the table — and an occasional catbird drops in for breakfast crumbs. Sit over there — no one faces you. You might as well be at the rail of a ship, for under your chin is the broad shimmering surface of the harbour, and you cannot see the rocks below. It's just as much fun to eat without facing somebody as it is to eat facing somebody. Especially Mary's curry of lobster.

One winter night there was a dinner in the red-and-black Octagon Room next door, and everything was suave and formal. Lord and Lady Gregory were there, and Amy Lowell and Henry James were there, and several other *aficionados* of words and victuals. "The only other character present under sixty and 180 pounds except myself," Sleeper related, "was a polite young Spanish professor from Harvard."

The talk, he said, was violently intellectual. "I really stuffed 'em," he chuckled. "By coffee and brandy there wasn't a female stay in the place, that wasn't creaking. To save their lives, the wonderful Aunt Amy Lowell (not smoking her cigar this night) suggested we all play games. So we played musical chairs, here in the Golden Step Room. After each pause in the music, and the rough-house scramble for chairs, the whole company rocked and yelled and wept with laughter. Some sat on the floor, because they could not rise. I thought I had a mass apoplexy on my hands with all those overfed elderly brains. After a few stanzas, the grave young Spaniard came to me and whispered:

" 'Señor Sleeper — may I make a suggestion? You are, of course, the host. But I think that *if* we had *just one more chair,* much of this confusion might be averted!' "

How they felt you know when you rise from the shipside-table here and crawl into the sun to sleep it off. Mary Wonson's food was pretty historic itself.

Someone always broke the siesta to ask: "Mr. Sleeper, could I really *see* the house?" Nothing pleased him more. A little guided tour would form up, as it does today.

It took an hour or longer. Every room is a mild ambush and a trap — either of objective design, or historical suggestion, or mischievous comfort, or all three. Back through the corridor to the central hall with its amber-glass showcase and the Connecticut door-ways and hot-Washington, the trail leads into a tiny passage not more than six-by-eight feet, lighted only from a flat skylight, and furnished surprisingly with a dainty brass-spangled mahogany escritoire, and good mezzotints, and smooth faintly-striped French paper, all as unlike the other moods of Beauport as well could be. The passage is a bon-bon — if a passage can be a bon-bon.

Your guide has a purpose in holding you imprisoned in this pleasant candy-box: the pause makes his next gesture the most effective. He suddenly flips open a narrow door, "Let's go in here"; and he propels you civilly into the next room. It may well be the climax of this incomparable house. Its contrast with the little candy-box passage is almost physical.

Here is the room which, if nothing else be saved forever, must somehow be. It is often called "the Pine Kitchen," and more formally the "Pembroke Room." It is in fact a reconstruction of the great serene cooking-eating-living-studying-praying room which was the central point of most of the earliest houses in New England. It is the true cell of the pioneer stock.

The Pembroke Room is L in shape, ample and rambling. Every square foot is composed in utility — a quality currently exploited loudly as "functional." Limited as the first settlers were in materials, and spare as they were in colour-appetite, the room's prevailing spectrum is all the tones of honest maple-sugar. Most everything, but the floor and the low overhead beams, is of a warm and faintly pinkish pine: the simple wall panels, the tables, the dressers and cupboards and shelves against the walls, the great wing chairs, the tall winged settle beside the large working fireplace, and the turned grille of the taproom doorway's half-door and bar-counter, complete with the yarbs and simples and spirits of pioneer medication. Myles Standish, in tall hat and homespun breeches, seems just to have stepped out, taking the gun from over the door as he left.

Sleeper's first maternal forebears on this side (the Westcott line) settled in the 17th century in Pembroke, down towards Cape Cod. Seven or eight generations had lived in the house. The legend runs that it had been sold at auction, shortly before Harry had his brainwave. He traced the auctioneer, borrowed his books of sale, and bought back, from every scattered purchaser, every object which had furnished the kitchen his own tribe had occupied for more than two centuries. He then summoned an ancient kinswoman with a camera eye, who as a girl had often visited the homestead and knew where every object had stood. Sleeper was now ready to build onto Beauport his ancestral hearth, with everything in its proper place. So he did. This is it.

The fireplace smoulders ready to kindle and cook, with all the irons and kittles and ovens clean. The dining-table in the ell is set with earthenware and homespun and horn-handled knives and forks. There is ink in the pot on the desk, and a quill to write with. There is fresh maple sugar in a jar, there are fresh red apples in pewter bowls, and there are edible dried apples and varied edible nuts in other jars. The musket is loaded for deer or tax collectors. No better meal was ever put away than one prepared entirely at the great hearth of this wonderful room. Even the herbs hang drying from the cornice beam. After you've eaten, on your long horse-ride from Plymouth to Boston (hence the taproom) you can just sit before the fire in a form-fitting pine-eared chair, with a candle on an adjustable ratchet beside you, and read Cotton Mather for a while. You will find it a suitable refuge from whatever ails you, no matter what ails you.

For those who like good pine, it may be noted here that this room is of pine-wood exclusively, but that the colour of the pine is not the bilious green-brown purveyed for bars, coffee-shoppes, or smoking-and-"rumpus"-rooms today. Nor is it the blanched chalk of the so-called "pickle" persuasion, nor is it the tipsy-owl-eyed "knotty" material which makes a wall look like a fence shot at with stewed prunes. It's just virgin pink-white "punkin" pine weathered in salt air for a couple of hundred years, dusted occasionally, and waxed by the hands of a few generations of hard-working Yankees. The same effect may be obtained with new pine by applying a diluted water solution of permanganate of potash to the right tone, to be followed by a once-over of pale shellac, to be followed by a scrub-down with a water solution of Fuller's earth. You can rub on a very little wax after that if you like, and don't say I never told you. (We are falling back of the tour; let's get going.)

"The place *is* incredible," someone says. "How did Mr. Sleeper go about it?"

He went about it as follows:

Mr. Sleeper conceived wholly *in his mind* a new room, perfect down to the last detail of a sand-blotter on a desk. Then he went about assembling it. Then he built it. That is all.

But how did he get the conception?

In strange ways.

A single object has been known to set off his fuse.

One day on Cambridge Street in Boston he asked a friend to drop in with him at a basement junk shop. The pal soon got bored and said let us get out of here. "Just a second," said Sleeper. He had found a crude and dusty wood-carving, obviously native, and was looking speculatively at it, fingers on his lips.

It appeared to be three carved and painted pine curtains, ample in their wooden folds, as crimson satin three inches thick, with golden rope tie-backs and tassels the size of Brünnehilde's pigtails. "Hmmmmmmmm . . ." he mused. "Those curtains mean pointed windows. Pointed windows mean a round room. Round room means tower on top. Maybe Norman tower, with a tile cap, like a silo or pigeon loft. Hmmmmmmmm."

"How long are you going to fool around here saying 'Hmmmmmmmm?'" asked his companion. "I am hungry."

"Thank you," said Mr. Sleeper to the junk dealer. "I'll take them." He bought for $12 a set of hand-carved painted pine window curtains, with carved tassels. They had originally decorated the inside of a fancy hearse. They cost him three new rooms, which cost him several thousand dollars, even when domestic building was possible.

Here before us is the result. We stand in the center of a two-story round stone tower, say 12 feet across. There is one window — a triptych really: hen-window in the middle, chicken-windows flank it. They are pointed, and the carved pine curtains frame them. The cylinder of the tower is lined with bookshelves. Just above our heads is a white-balustered gallery, with a mahogany rail; over the rail hangs one of the few, almost vanished battle-flags bearing the legend: AN APPEAL TO HEAVEN, and a pine tree, and the date 1776. The cylinder-tower is solid with unusual books. At the window is a little desk, and on it a manuscript letter, and a pair of steel-rimmed glasses. You can sit there in solitude and peer out through the trees toward Norman's Woe. None of this would have happened if he had not blundered into that junk shop in a Boston cellar.

Many of his conceptions started with collections, and his collections often started not with a batch but with a single piece. He had the eye of a hawk for things of beauty

9

at no matter how trifling a price. Long before things came into "vogue" — that is to say, got caught in the up-bidding of the junk and antique and decorating trades — he was picking them up here and there for the proverbial first line of a song. That is why you, too, with strong legs, a good eye, and a little persistence, can make any wall of your one-room prefabricated residence unusual and as satisfying as any wall in Beauport. And that is what you may as well start doing the moment you leave Gloucester.

Sleeper wasn't remotely interested in vogues, nor in collections as possessions; groups of related or contrasting things simply provoked unusual rooms, unusual arrangements and thus unusual and cherishable moods.

The whole house, unlike the unconventional "Colonial restoration" is *not* white. It is a symphony of subtle colours, effected mostly by paint, a consummate use of fabrics of widely varying tones and generally small patterns, of small bits of exceptional wallpaper, and of furniture, objects and prints each of which is a pleasing thing; many of which then cost very little, and some of which are noble as well as affordable today. "So many people," he once said, "overlook the fact that once our ancestors had struggled out of their early harsh life, they cheered up and slapped colour on everything in reach." That's one reason why the experts from the Metropolitan Museum who were planning the new and vastly successful American Wing spent a couple of weeks here at Beauport just blotting up ideas and hospitality, and making notes. That's why you'll observe Sleeper's idiom in arrangement in room after room since created all over America by the notable decorators who knew, liked and studied the man and his work, and by their own artistic heirs.

Antique dealers had for Sleeper, the man, a respect way above and beyond the normal truckling of commerce. They rarely tried to stick him, for they knew they would never stick him twice. They quoted him their best prices because to say that he was their client gave plausible intensity to the positively-true-blue of their integrity. He would race through their shops, pointing to this and that, knowing where each piece would fit a precise gap in the jig-saw puzzle of room-plans he carried all in his head. The old and honest dealers today light candles for him, and though they serve and respect the prominent decorators who honour him, they all agree there is none to take Sleeper's special place.

We could easily use a long time in a tour of the upper floors, with its crazy roofs making steep angles of the walls, and pointing or eliminating flat ceilings. Let's try.

The amplest of them is the Strawberry Hill bedroom. Two of its walls are covered clear to the apex with a green paper, lacquered almost black, sprigged with parti-coloured groups of triumphant Orientals on elephants and camels — a paper inspired by one in Horace Walpole's house at Strawberry Hill, in Twickenham. The bed is a carven maple four-poster, the hooked rug a rich riot of flowers on a dark floor thinly spattered with the other tones of the room. A neighboring bedroom is papered in a great sprawling Chinese vine, to the ceiling; the woodwork is apple green, two giant urns of apple-green Bristol stand sentry on pedestals in its long bow window. One wall-panel (bearing a dark landscape painting) swings out to disclose a generous mirror. In no bedroom are the flotsam and jetsam of restless living apparent; the zigzag walls are honeycombed with invisible clothes closets, one of which is literally up a pair of steep steps inside the wall of the tiny room which has Byron's own bed in it. For years I hunted in vain for a secret passage between the two main wings of the house; I was sure the floor-lines left a gap somewhere; I still suspect there is one, but I am probably wrong — though only the other day I first found an unsuspected closet with a staircase going up to nowhere. I suspected hidden rooms because downstairs, in the wall of the Jacobean Room which was taken bodily from the witchcraft days of Salem, and from a house associated with witchcraft, there *is* a real and secret half-circular staircase. "That," said Harry, "is so that when the mob comes to seize Aunt Imprudence, to duck her for a witch, we can spirit her upstairs. The old gal probably deserves a first-class ducking."

We could also kill a little time in a sitting-room which was garnished with an early American piano, and a set of Ackermann's repository, and early Edinburgh Reviews. Or visit in a large bedroom of fragrant natural pine, with two field beds, five pine cupboards filled with books and primitive Yankee toys, and a window-seat looking out to sea. From this "Indian Room" it is a step through a fanlit doorway to a pine attic-room from Providence, the Mariner's Room, with charts and a quadrant, with old copies of the Essex newspaper on the table, and a fine spyglass view of the harbour entrance from a huge strategic Windsor reading chair. Or we could relax on the North Gallery's porch overlooking the harbour, as the present King and Queen of Sweden did one afternoon and murmured: "Ah, this is so like home." But we've only time for two or three more rooms; let's go back downstairs.

The first is another tiny bedroom painted a vague dusty grey green and called the Chapel Chamber, or the Paul Revere Room. A canopy bed, a dressing table, a highboy, and a corner cupboard are its chief objects. The ceiling tapers to a Gothic peak. The walls are papered with a famous Christopher-Wren-church design copied off the the walls of Paul Revere's own house in Boston. On the ledge of one pointed window stood a small wooden replica of the Old North Church in Salem Street, which is now in the Otis House in Boston. The interior of the corner cupboard is painted a dirty pink, with a scalloped thin valance of mulberry chintz — against the pink once shone a lavish collection of original Paul Revere silver, which you don't pick up for a verse and two choruses any more. Sleeper gave most of it to the Boston Museum of Fine Arts, where you may see it in a room dedicated to Maria Westcott, his mother.

The second is a long, narrow good-natured living-room. The South Gallery, it's called. The gabled window-alcove at the harbour-end is shelved for coloured "witch-balls" of glass that flicker in the sun. The long thin room is panelled from an old house — even including two sealed fireplaces — and is painted a warm chocolate brown. And there is a table-arrangement for which Mr. Chamberlain's camera speaks most succinctly and eloquently.

The third is a room that is as unexpected to the general orchestration of the house, as well a room may be.

It started life as a two-story, bleak, stony, forbidding Puritan sort of chapel. Then one summer it was curtained off for awhile. When the magician lifted the curtain under which he had concealed the Puritan chapel, it had vanished. One saw instead the most startling and elegant fragment of a Chinese hall that was ever taken spiritually — if not bodily — from the old Empress' apartments in the Imperial Palace in Peking.

11

It is some thirty-five feet long, twenty-five high, fifteen wide, with a ceiling shaped up like the inside of a pagoda. Upon all the walls is a vivid Chinese hand-painted scenic paper depicting the arts and crafts of China; this is believed to have been imported for the new house of Lewis Morris, but he never used it; and it lay unopened in the attic of the Gerry House in Marblehead, where Sleeper found it in its original boxes, seasoned for a century or so, and put it up here.

"You see," he said, "these boys used to set out from Salem round the Horn, pick up otter skins in the Northwest, sail to Honolulu for sandalwood, then on to China to trade their cargoes for silk and tea and spices. Sam Morison says the average age of the China-trade skipper was only around twenty or twenty-one — that is, when he sailed from here. Out in Hongkong and Shanghai and Foochow they'd pick up gifts for their best girls at home. That's how Chestnut Street in Salem became, for a time, almost an Oriental museum. Things like that get sold and dispersed. I've been picking them up here and there for years. I just thought we ought to have a room to recollect that brave period. Our best girls are just as pretty today."

He certainly got what he aimed for. Mrs. McCann developed it into a Chinese Chippendale drawing-room of formalized luxury. The jeweled tapestry of the wallpaper is interrupted only by fine Chippendale mahogany pieces, a complex madder-and-cream carven Italianate mantlepiece of marble, and golden fretwork galleries above the mullioned-windows at both ends. After dark a huge writhing Waterford chandelier spills a bouquet of candle-light upon the unbelievable total.

Through a sequence of accidents too long to relate, Sleeper found in California, a new circle of acolytes. His trips to the Far West became more frequent as the warmth of his friendships expanded, and as the demand for his genius rose. He was to be in California all summer in 1934. Suddenly he fell ill, and came East at once, but not to Gloucester — he went feet first to the Phillips House, a hospital in Boston. He never saw Beauport again.

Tentative offers flowed in for piecemeal parts of this ship-built, interlocked, integrated masterpiece. A collector wanted the Octagon Room, another the Chinese Room, another bought a rare collection of amber. A dealer wanted the Pembroke Room. One collector wanted the tower library intact. The executor was tilting toward acceptance when another of those predestined things happened.

Mr. and Mrs. Charles E. F. McCann of New York came to Gloucester to visit. They thereupon did just what we have been doing in these pages. "This house and collection," said Mrs. McCann, "must be preserved." She bought it.

No more sympathetic owner could have taken over. Its responsibility was her joy. If Mrs. McCann and Henry Sleeper had been permitted to live, they would have written this book as it should be written.

Everything that really counts in the strange history of Beauport is in place. The Stiegel glass, with Stiegel's own framed indenture-paper above it, is still in the tiny passage off the kitchen. The "Reward-of-Merit" cards on the corner desk of the Mariner's Room lie casually there today. The gulls are wheeling as usual, and the Gloucestermen make out for the Banks, and the lobstermen haul their early pots just offshore. Nothing important is changed.

BEAUPORT FROM THE AIR

Since this book, like Sleeper's life, is primarily a tour of interiors, you'll find in it no other outdoor view but this, taken from an airplane which Samuel Champlain never even suspected in 1604. It shows the ruddy granite ledge from which Beauport's syncopation of roof-lines piles up against the summer sky. Compare the picture with the end-papers of this book and you may find out where you are — though this is not compulsory in a house of enchantment, with at least eight chimneys and more gables than you can shake Nathaniel Hawthorne at. From the chairs on the lower terrace, center, you command the full arc of the Harbour, with Gloucester to starboard, the reef of Norman's Woe and the breakwater to port. Pronging into the lower picture is a landing, with submarine steps leading to the habitat of lobsters, a time-honoured and savory Gloucester product.

THE COGSWELL ROOM

Here is where we enter, where Beauport began its growth around panelling from the William Cogswell House in nearby Essex. The notable trumpet-leg cabinet (left) houses Chinese Export porcelain made for a Portuguese noble, from Mrs. McCann's collection. A harlequin hooked rug softens the waxed-brick floor.

THE GREEN DINING-ROOM

All woodwork in this "first dining-room" is painted the green of the back of a laurel leaf, the floor is dark waxed-brick. The graceful Adam mirror picks up the copper on the ledge of the east wall.

On the gate-leg table: a double-octagon framed fantasy of a million sea-shells, twin lamps, dark lacquer tray, rare sprigged tea set. The arched door opens on a shell-cupboard loaded with collector's china.

Ceramic ladies and pewter lamps preside over three examples of the amazing McCann collection of Chinese Export porcelain now shared by the Boston Museum of Fine Arts, and New York's Metropolitan.

Wrought iron torch-candles repeat the flicker of the fire in the black brick grate. The arch-door (right) opens from the Cogswell Room, echoing the arch of the china cupboard we just saw.

A sharp note of colour contrast to the cool green is this handsome glass-matted, gold-framed sanguine portrait by Saint Memin, fringed on the black ledge by a sifting of pewter and two green tole candlesticks.

General Washington, hollow, complete with toga, scroll, hat and sword, is an old Albany stove of most realistic warmth. His escorting eagles are repeated on the painted chair-top.

A Connecticut doorway set bodily in the wall displays 130 specimens of brown and amber glass, the light playing through their tapestry from ground glass. The "bull's eyes" are 24 Sandwich cup-plates.

As if one doorway were not enough, a second (left) becomes a cabinet for more old glass, lavender and green and pink. The desk is of curly maple. The panelling is made of old window blinds.

The woodwork is all a juicy cocoa brown; the wallpaper a Chinese arabesque, light flowers on cocoa. The floor is finely spattered. A Chippendale mirror and glass-paintings above a four-drawer maple chest brighten the alcove.

(Right) A one-turn staircase leads up to the Strawberry Hill, Byron, and Nelson Rooms. At a wall-niche on the landing you pause to inspect an unusual early coloured engraving of Mont St. Michel, and to covet, below it, a group of romantic Staffordshire figurines, one of whom is a sailor, reclining, fatigued, upon a mossy bank.

A watchman guards the passage to the Octagon Room.

THE OCTAGON ROOM

The background of this pointed window is ground glass. Its shelves and mullions frame thirty pieces of amethyst glass, from lightest lavender to deepest Concord-grape.

THE OCTAGON ROOM

Left to right: Doorway and window (p. 24); floral Portuguese wool draperies; tall red-lacquer screen; great square-front maple sideboard, against a vivid pattern of sparkling scarlet tôle-ware.

The noble sideboard commands this view; across the octagonal center-table we glimpse the pantry-passage filled with tole and red-and-blue glass. Colour fairly sings against the plum-black walls.

Nowhere is shape and symmetry in arrangement of variety better "mapped" than on the sideboard in the Octagon Room. Whether you collect teacups or toy fire engines this use of wall-space must be an inspiration.

(Left) The fireplace (black, with brass) supports another perfect pattern: oval pastel portrait, silhouettes, vermilion bindings, lobster-red tole candles and brackets, and urns.

The amber-gold of striped maple, the plum-black of all woodwork (lightly lined in lacquer-red), floral fabrics and rugs, vermilion in bindings and tôle-ware: that is the warm, rich colour-scheme.

(Opposite) Each room you enter echoes the one you leave: This pantry passage is bright with the Octagon's red—but its windows stage two rich batteries of glass, not only red but deep blue, for transition to the cooler light beyond.

(Above) Similarly, the sharp transition to the white Golden Step Room is prepared for you by the amethyst glass window and (right) the "echoing" morocco volumes. Note the uncommon Aaron Willard clock on the passage wall.

THE GOLDEN STEP

Dominated, nay christened, by this walloping model of the square-rigger *Golden Step,* this white-walled, cool indoor terrace is the perfect summer dining-room. Its shelves bear green Wedgewood and English majolica. Two long white dining-tables with Windsor and tall-back chairs are of the simplest carpenter-dignity. The window-side table commands a 180-degree view of the harbour.

(Right) The arched blind window is flanked by ship-carvings of mermen wrestling with tropical fruit.

Yonder is the door through which we entered — screened, for the windows slide down on fresh days. A Gloucester "pinky" perches high on the wall and a wooden-sailed half-model sails above the firebreast.

The globes hold aquamarine "witch balls" and coloured glass marbles. In the cabinet, gilt tableware. The *Golden Step* sits on an ancient Chinese bench. The iron blackamoor by the door rings a bell, quite loudly.

THE PEMBROKE ROOM

Probably nowhere on earth will you find a more sympathetic reconstruction of the heart of the pioneer home, family, community, than here in the room which Sleeper reassembled from the oak-and-pine house of his forebears at Pembroke—after it had been dispersed at auction. The heart of the room is its huge and hospitable working hearth, its hand-made utensils racked above.

The tall fireside settle (left) curves inward to trap warmth and toast shins. Oak posts and beams, pine walls, and chimney brick are the room's basic materials. Deep in the fireplace are ovens and warming-ledges. On a crane hangs a noble iron kettle.

At the left is the tripod candlestand for reading the Scripture. Spices on the shelf, bellows and salt-box, buckets and bowls and fire-irons . . . each in its proper place.

Here, nearly three centuries ago, gathered the typical Yankee family — here in winter its children were born, its meals prepared year-round, its courtin' eavesdropped, its neighbors welcomed, its prayers said.

The Pembroke Room is L-shaped. The view above follows the staff of the ell past the fireplace to a dining-table, backed by a tall pine sideboard filled with Colonial earthenware. Note the graceful sweep of the solid pine wing-chair, mercifully cushioned with homespun pillows.

(Left) Two of the earliest chairs of their type are gossiping. Those who proclaim that Puritans never knew rocking-chairs will be reminded that this room accumulated new and different utilities over a span of 250 years—and kept its character. There is probably a patriotic lesson in that fact.

THE PEMBROKE ROOM

Warm, faintly rose-amber pine walls; austere hardwood chairs and table; broad pine floors — and for colour, two gay martial painted roller-shades, and small-pattern narrow madder and yellow chintzes.

Facing the sideboard (p. 36) is another with pewter cups gleaming against early glazed earthenware of coppery brown. An eagle perches on the slant-front cupboard (right). Pistol and musket are handy.

The half-door is the bar of the taproom where riders, Plymouth-or-Boston-bound, relaxed with a drink not too soft. A cranberry rake hangs above it and a mammoth pine corner-cupboard stands next to it.

The long view west along the foot of the ell. The table is set. A saddler's bench will do for one chair. A tidy Windsor wash-handstand (right) was useful before mealtime if the cranberry bog was muddy.

Another view of the foot of the ell. A children's table is at the far end. Above the wash-stand at the left is an unusual mirror for both tall and short. The door at the left leads to the Franklin Room.

This wing chair, designed by Mr. Sleeper, was built of fragrant "punkin" pine by the patriarch Poole over in Gloucester . . . said he "didn't believe in worm holin'" . . . said, "my worms all went on strike."

The "children's table" for intimate meals, is lighted by a tin-cone candelabrum and from above, a nail-pierced lantern. Two more patriotic shades strike a Yankee Doodle note.

(Right) The same table, as it is set for luncheon, with warm sun streaming in from the garden.

(Opposite) A study in textures: a corner cupboard in the Pembroke Room, and its collection of working pottery, including an acrobatic goose.

In the (literally) 2 x 4-foot passage from Pembroke to Franklin hangs this framed indenture concerning Stiegel and his glass. It is only fitting that the glass in the narrow shelves is Stiegel's.

THE FRANKLIN ROOM

The walls, ochre brown; window hangings, turkey red calico, tied with brass; the floor cheerful with rugs. Benjamin Franklin's own-made stove is yonder, with his bas-relief cast into it.

The opposite view, across the checker table. Gold and black painted chairs, an ivory yarn-reel, swagged and tasseled curtains, painted shades, mahogany tables, composed in Franklin's own "who-cares" idiom.

THE JACOBEAN ROOM

An ample drop-leaf table in the bay window reflects the diamond sunshine that lights this impressive dark-oak room of the "witchcraft" mood.

The long view of the Jacobean Room: pale pewter forms a silvery constellation in the dresser. The far narrow panel hides the fugitive witches' secret spiral staircase. The early Victorian doll-carriage is where doll carriages most often are—out of place, and underfoot.

(Right) Two cast-iron Redskins warm themselves at the blaze.

A splendid little oaken Jacobean cabinet (in an alcove dictated by steampipes) holds good pewter; a gate-cupboard above it holds still more. The chair is unique—but your "little man" could copy it.

THE CHINESE ROOM

THE CHINESE ROOM

Mrs. McCann transformed this extraordinary room from its next-earlier incarnation (still earlier it had been a chapel), into the opulent Georgian-Chippendale drawing room you see here. It is "keyed" by a unique hand-painted Chinese paper imported, but unused, for the mansion of Lewis Morris, the "Signer." It lay fresh and hidden in the attic of a Marblehead house for over a century. The furniture today is of English pedigree. Carved and pierced gold screens serve as rails for the twin galleries at either end. The ceiling curves in-and-upward to the rooftree, as in a pagoda. The chandelier is of fairly unbelievable Waterford.

The wide view, looking towards the glazed window cabinet with its fretted shelves. Details of the wallpaper depict, in bright colours on a bluish ground, the arts and sciences of China.

(Right) This English secretary proves to be a superb example of the harmony between things western and eastern.

Years—perhaps the lifetimes of many Chinese painters—went into this famous wallpaper, of which we see here a five-foot detail. It is a document of record in classic antique books.

(Above) The overmantel scene shows potters making ceramics at their furnaces.

(Left) The enlarged detail depicts the growing, reaping, and threshing of rice.

THE CHAPEL CHAMBER (or PAUL REVERE ROOM)—Sleeper's collection of Paul Revere silver, now in the Boston Museum, once filled the cabinet. The paper is from Paul Revere's house in Boston.

THE SOUTH GALLERY—On a satinwood and mahogany Sheraton table is this incomparable symmetry of black glass urns, red volumes glinting gold, two clear-glass candy jars, three Stafford busts, a gold lyre clock with eagle panel from Currier & Foster's vanished shop in Salem. The classic engravings are in colour; the panelling of the whole room is painted the brown of the skin of a good pumpkin pie. It's a long, sunny room, facing the harbour through a festoon of particoloured "witch" globes.

THE PINEAPPLE ROOM

In the passage that links the South Gallery and the Tower Library one pauses to inspect and sigh. The wallpaper, in the lightest possible viridian on white, shows fruit-groups and animal landscapes divided by bamboo poles supporting each a pine-apple. On one wall the Contriver hung a toile-de-Jouy showing William Penn making a deal with the Indians. Upon it are displayed two framed pre-Audubon birds, and a cross of positive and negative silhouettes.

In this setting are such items as a tall secretary, and (left) a shell-cupboard in white, lively with pale bottles against green—against ladies' fancy fans.

THE TOWER LIBRARY

These are the carved wooden hearse-curtains that "caused" this whole cylinder of books, 12 feet wide, 16 tall. A hidden stair sneaks up to the balcony, with its Pine Tree flag. A round hooked rug is on the floor.

THE SHELLEY ROOM

What to do with an attic: paper it all-over oyster-white traced in faint lavender. Use mulberry window-chintzes, a lavender bedspread on the four-poster. Cut a pointed triptych into the gable. Toss a few Concord-grape-colour books around. If you're a lady who loved Shelley too much (Sleeper said this room was for her) put a bunch of magenta zinnias in a purple vase.

(Left) Much in little space — the Willow Room, with a bed, table, dresser, closet, bath, two sunlit windows . . . and who needs more, pray?

THE BYRON ROOM—From the door you see Lord Byron's own bed, from Newstead Abbey, let into the slope of Beauport's roof. The paper is a genteel pastoral of brown-and-yellow on white.

Facing the door we came in: a mahogany dresser, gold Federal mirror, geometrical hooked rug and a sea-captain's travelling folding desk. The panelling is ochre-brown.

THE NELSON ROOM

Toile framing the window above shows Marie Antoinette "cutting up," and in exactly the right place, over Nelson's bedside lamp, is a miniature of Lady Hamilton. The wallpaper is a quiet diamond pattern in brown on ivory. The panelling is painted a darker brown.

(Left) On so simple a premise as a square of toile-de-Jouy depicting Lord Nelson's funeral cortège, this charming snug bedroom became a "personage." The toile hangs above the satinwood dressing table.

THE BELFRY BEDROOM

Splashing dancing morning sunlight makes lace on the spattered floor and floral rug as Chinese vines and flowers climb the green bird-cage walls of this bower. Bouquets of garden flowers accent the white chintz at four windows. Bed, dresser and dressing table are of striped maple, of course. A door-panel hides an ample closet.

(Left) Need a mirror? Just push the knob on this painting of a seaport belfry. The panel opens wide on an ample glass.

The four-poster snuggles under the gable, with plenty of headroom, and a reading-lantern hangs at exactly the right point overhead. The bedspread is of a pedigreed woven design, which you may copy.

A perfect example of what to do with "angles you can't do anything with": into a sharp low gable fits a maple dresser, a gilt-and-black mirror, a row of favorite books, and a conviction of your own personality.

In Haiti they build half-houses; why not a half-room? This is your view from your bed to the door that leads into the equally fabulous Strawberry Hill Room, a dark-green contrast to your light-green tent.

THE STRAWBERRY HILL ROOM

On the preceding page we were looking back into the Belfry Room, through the vertical half-door. Here once more two walls climb to a ridge-pole papered, in this instance, with a dark rich lacquered pattern inspired from Strawberry Hill. Its story is an endless pageant of elephants and kings and camels. At the left (above and below) we see the gable ends of the room, painted a dark, dark brown picked out in red. Overhead, William confronts Mary. Below, a maple bureau, a girandole, a tall maple clock and a portrait share honours. The four-post bed sports a Paisley gown on its foot-rail. The rug is a pot pourri of blossoms.

The corner holds a delightful little table of exquisite craftsmanship. The blue-and-white tin chandelier overhead makes twilight fireworks. (Better take your parasol.)

No room without its heat, or diversion. A greyhound tops this convex mirror, not disturbed by the Hessian andirons, nor the warming pan. The slim panel at the right of grandfather's clock conceals a large hidden closet of ancient costumes and a stair which leads up exactly nowhere at all.

(Left) Turn right now and regard the pattern of the dresser-top arrangement, the Stafford in the red-fringed shelves, the tinkle-lamps, and the admirable portrait of a good-looking school boy supposed always to have been young Harry Sleeper, but affectionately claimed as kin by several other estimable visitors.

The little dressing-table is black, lined in yellow; its sidelights are brass lamps with etched cranberry-glass globes on marbleized-bases. Horace Walpole, himself, peeps through the tracery of the chandelier.

THE UPSTAIRS SITTING ROOM

In a tiny sitting room next to Strawberry Hill is a saucy satinwood and mahogany square piano, by Hayes Babcock and Appleton of No. 6 Milk Street, Boston. A clear Sandwich lamp lights the music, which is *The Haydn*. A nearby bookshelf holds a casual sixty volumes of *The Edinburgh Review* of the early 1800's. The French and English prints are in colour—as is the glass. The wallpaper is quietly striped.

Let's be frank: there isn't a house, large or small, that hasn't some such casual wall as this, and some sort of dresser, chest and a pair of decent chairs, and some pleasant prints (or a thrifty print shop nearby). This simple arrangement can be anyone's, and to his personal taste or hobby. Add a few timely flowers for the finger-vases, or your own, and the whole becomes a picture you painted yourself. Get to work.

THE INDIAN ROOM

Real architectural complexity is reduced to simplicity by the fact that floor, ceiling, walls and furniture are of "natural" wood-colour, weathered and waxed, and that the few fabrics compose in tone to the subtle, bland whole. The canopies of the twin-poster beds were tailored to the roof-line to save floor space (which is generous). Everything that belongs out of sight is hidden. Everything in sight is an object of interest. *Item:* Framed Bill of Sale of the Negro Boy "Mink," 1804. (Mink died 1863). *Items:* (they're on that wall) Four prints of Robinson Crusoe. *Item:* The first print of America's first railroad. Engine named *John Bull,* Albany-Schenectady run, scared hell out of the cows. *Item:* An 8 x 10 pink and blue floral hooked rug, oval, and scalloped. *Item:* Gloucester sea chest, labelled the property of A. Marchant. And so on. . . .

Between the beds a low maple dresser for two holds reading lamps against a painted roller-shade. The frills and spreads are a cocoa-brown printed in feathers on off-white; the roof broods protectively.

Open the cupboard beside the door to the Mariner's room and you'll find two shelves of primitive wooden pioneer toys of the beasts they loved best—the barnyard folk, in wood. The cradle is for a guest.

Lie in bed and rest facing this calm design: plain virgin pine, wearing fleurets of wiggling hinges. The double-rocker (right) is said to have been for sparkin' couples. Sort of rumble-seat, early model.

Lo, the poor Indian.

Mrs. Lo, hence the Indian Room.

THE MARINER'S ROOM

We just came down those steps on the previous page, almost missed the pine desk, the pickwick, the steeple-model in the oval window, the half-written letters, the blue-homespun valance. For we face this (above): a full-panoplied Rhode Island doorway, long table, open on it a copy of the Essex paper with a full front-page story of the Battle of Lake Erie (issue of Sept. 10, 1814, or *Don't Give Up The Ship*). Bright rippled tin candle-sconces flank the door. As in the Indian Room, the "finish" of the wood is *none* but time and wax. To be sure, the pine brackets (left) are harmonious, and you can make them, and yours will look well another 200 years.

A close-up of the rhythm and line of the far doorway in the Mariner's Room.

If Washington can get hot downstairs, so can this lyre-and-eagle stove cast by Groma and Low. (Washington is represented by a hexagonal plaque in the gable-panel above, but we can't see him.)

You'll not overlook on the table the compass, or the scrimshaw marlinspike, or the scrimshaw cribbage board . . . nor, on the round table, the quadrant, nor the astronomical gadget that looks like an egg-beater. A spy-glass lies there too, for looking out for Gloucestermen overdue. They may not, in fact, come home at all.

(Right) A formal corner desk for learning to keep strict account, a pine school-desk. Good sailing is sound schooling.

In the cupboards beyond the Mariner's long table (above) you may discover a collection of carved and painted Indians, a foot high, twenty carved miniature birds, one carved speckled trout, and a wooden figure of an English marine carved in China, in 1840. Among other matters you'll inspect Andrew Jackson's passport to a New Bedford ship (1837), a sextant made by Spenser Browning and Rust in London for Sam'l Emery in Salem, facsimiles of Washington's account books of the Revolution, a box of German toy blocks with the card of J. Henry Sleeper, 1840 . . . and some Reward-of-Merit cards, awarded to Harry Sleeper by an admirer. He deserved them.

A feminine touch in this seaman's room is suddenly revealed in the little niche (left) with its carriage bonnet and blue boxes.

THE NORTH GALLERY

Gallery? Yes. The shelves of the cases are filled, pane by pane, with exquisite little books open to colour prints of birds, beasts, flowers. The pilasters wear heads of Washington, Lafayette, Franklin, Jefferson. A mother eagle feeds her young. Chairs of the type Jerome Bonaparte brought here stand under Montgolfier's balloon ascension in Paris—which Franklin witnessed.

INDEX

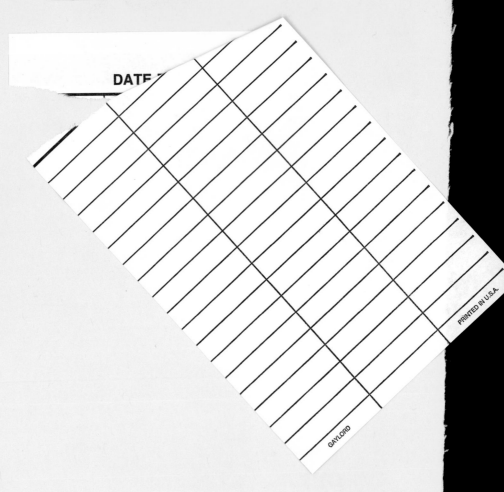

DATE

GAYLORD

PRINTED IN U.S.A.